WHO IS THIS MAN

Resources by John Ortberg

An Ordinary Day with Jesus
(curriculum with Ruth Haley Barton)

Everybody's Normal Till You Get to Know Them
(book, audio)

God Is Closer Than You Think
(book, audio, curriculum with Stephen and Amanda Sorenson)

If You Want to Walk on Water,
You've Got to Get Out of the Boat
(book, audio, curriculum with Stephen and Amanda Sorenson)

Know Doubt
(book, formerly entitled *Faith and Doubt*)

The Life You've Always Wanted
(book, audio, curriculum with Stephen and Amanda Sorenson)

Living the God Life

Love Beyond Reason

The Me I Want to Be
(book, audio, curriculum with Scott Rubin)

Teaching the Heart of the Old Testament and
Truth for Today from the Old Testament series
(book, curriculum with Kevin and Sherry Harney)

When the Game Is Over, It All Goes Back in the Box
(book, audio, curriculum with Stephen and Amanda Sorenson)

JOHN ORTBERG
WITH CHRISTINE M. ANDERSON

WHO IS THIS MAN

The Unpredictable Impact
of the Inescapable Jesus

ZONDERVAN®

ZONDERVAN.com/
AUTHORTRACKER
follow your favorite authors

ZONDERVAN

Who Is This Man? Study Guide
Copyright © 2012 by John Ortberg

This title is also available as a Zondervan ebook.
Visit www.zondervan.com/ebooks.

Requests for information should be addressed to:

Zondervan, *Grand Rapids, Michigan* 49530

ISBN 978-0-310-68936-2

Cover design: *Extra Credit Projects*
Cover photography: *Jupiter Images*
Interior design: *Matthew Van Zomeren*

Printed in the United States of America

13 14 15 16 17 18 19 /DCI/ 20 19 18 17 16 15 14 13 12 11 10 9 8 7 6 5 4

CONTENTS

ABOUT THIS STUDY

I am continually drawn to this person Jesus. The more I learn about him—who he was, the way he lived, what he taught—the deeper my admiration for him becomes.

From complete obscurity, Jesus came to public attention for the blink of an eye—maybe three years, maybe as few as one. When he died, his tiny failed movement appeared clearly at an end. But Jesus' impact was greater a hundred years after his death than during his life; it was greater still after five hundred years; and after two thousand years he has more followers in more places than ever.

The complexity, depth, and power of his life are unique and unprecedented. In some ways, our biggest challenge in gauging his influence is that we take for granted the ways in which the world has been shaped by him. As you will soon discover, his vision of life has impacted the development of everything from art and science to government, medicine, and education.

Just as amazing as his impact on the world at large is the revolutionary way he treated individual human beings. When you consider the limitations and prejudices of the ancient world, you realize how remarkable it is that Jesus transcends them all. He treasured children, honored women, and had compassion on the suffering—none of whom were esteemed in his culture. Values we admire today such as humility and forgiveness were scorned and considered weaknesses in the ancient world. In Jesus' day, everyone knew the gods favored the rich and powerful—it was unthinkable that every human being was loved equally by God and therefore should be treated with dignity. But Jesus doesn't take a wrong step. His life and message are as relevant and challenging today as they were more than two thousand years ago.

How is this possible? *Who is this man?*

Whatever you know or think about Jesus, I invite you to take the steps you need to take to know him better. Rearrange your life if you have to. Getting to know any person well is a wonderful thing. Getting to know Jesus better is immensely rewarding—and almost always life changing. If you consider yourself a stranger to Jesus, I invite you to become his acquaintance. As you get to know him better, chances are good you will become an admirer—and admirers of Jesus have a natural tendency to become followers of Jesus. If you consider yourself a follower of Jesus already, I invite you to set aside your assumptions and look at Jesus as if you did not know anything about him. You might be surprised at what you discover.

This is a challenging study. It's about what matters most in life and in history, and how deeply those things are connected to our everyday lives. Don't settle for being a passive spectator. Take the risk of active engagement; wrestle with questions; open yourself to new ideas. Every investment you make—of time, energy, critical thinking, and personal vulnerability—will be well worth the effort. That's a promise—one I can make from personal experience.

My hope and prayer is that you not only come to know Jesus much, much better, but that your heart will beat faster with joy, gratitude, and awe that such a life got lived in this world. And in the process, I pray you will discover in Jesus a deeper understanding of the possibilities and significance of your own life.

John Ortberg

HOW TO USE THIS GUIDE

Group Size

This video curriculum is designed to be experienced in a group setting such as a Bible study, Sunday school class, or any small group gathering. To ensure everyone has enough time to participate in discussions, it is recommended that large groups break up into smaller groups of four to six people each.

Materials Needed

Each participant should have his or her own participant's guide, which includes outlines for the video segments, activities, and discussion questions, as well as personal studies to deepen learning between sessions. A copy of John Ortberg's book *Who Is This Man?* (one per person or couple), though not required for the group gathering, is a valuable asset for the personal study.

Timing

The time notations — for example (17 minutes) — indicate the *actual* time of video segments and the *suggested* times for each activity or discussion. For example:

Individual Activity: What I Want to Remember (2 minutes)

Adhering to the suggested times will enable you to complete each session in one hour. If you have a longer meeting, you may wish to allow more time for discussion and activities. You may also opt to devote two meetings rather than one to each session. In addition to allowing discussions to be more spacious, this has the added advantage of allowing group members to read related chapters in the *Who Is This Man?* book and to complete the personal study between meetings. In the second meeting, devote the time allotted for watching the video to discussing group members' insights and questions from their reading and personal study.

Facilitation

Each group should appoint a facilitator who is responsible for starting the video and for keeping track of time during discussions and activities. Facilitators may also read questions aloud and monitor discussions, prompting participants to respond and ensuring that everyone has the opportunity to participate.

Personal Studies

Maximize the impact of the curriculum with additional study between group sessions. Every personal study includes reflection questions, Bible study, and a guided prayer activity. You'll get the most out of the curriculum by setting aside about an hour between sessions for personal study (not including the suggested reading from the *Who Is This Man?* book). For each session, you may wish to complete the personal study all in one sitting or to spread it out over a few days.

THE MAN WHO WON'T GO AWAY

I am an historian, I am not a believer, but I must confess as an historian that this penniless preacher from Nazareth is irrevocably the very center of history.   H. G. WELLS

Welcome!

Welcome to Session 1 of *Who Is This Man?* If this is your first time together as a group, take a moment to introduce yourselves to each other before watching the video.

Video: The Man Who Won't Go Away (17 minutes)

Play the video segment for Session 1. As you watch, use the outline (pages 12 – 13) to follow along or to take notes on anything that stands out to you.

Notes

Jesus' impact on human history has been without parallel.

His presence is unavoidable.

His influence is inescapable.

His appeal is inexhaustible.

His endurance is inextinguishable.

The personal question: *How would you like Jesus to impact your life?*

This week:

- Take one of the things Jesus taught and allow it to shape your life: love your enemies; turn the other cheek; pursue reconciliation.

- Live in a spirit of humility: serve in a way you normally wouldn't serve, or remember someone who is poor and be generous with your money.

Group Discussion (41 minutes)

Take a few minutes to talk about what you just watched.

1. What part of the teaching had the most impact on you?

Inescapable Influence

2. On the video, John described the pervasive influence Jesus has had across history and on every sphere of life — art, science, government, medicine, education, social welfare, culture, philosophy, human rights (treatment of women, children, the poor and suffering), and more.

- Of all the progress and revolutionary changes John talked about that can be traced back to Jesus, which do you think have become so woven into the fabric of contemporary life and culture that they are now perhaps taken for granted?

- When you consider the ways Jesus has changed the world over time, which sphere of life stands out as one that has especially benefitted you? Share the reasons for your choice. For example, if you or someone in your family were born sick or with an obvious physical impairment, in ancient times you might have been killed or left to die of exposure. Knowing this, you might identify Jesus' influence on medicine or the treatment of children as especially beneficial to you.

Revolutionary Teaching

3. People who listened to Jesus were amazed and surprised by what he taught (Matthew 7:28 – 29). They said things like, "How did this man get such learning?" and, "No one ever spoke the way this man does" (John 7:15, 46).

Review on Your Own

Briefly review the ten revolutionary teachings of Jesus listed in the left column of the chart on pages 16 – 17.

- Place a ✓ next to one or two teachings you have recently witnessed being lived out among others in your own Christian community.

- Place a ✗ next to one or two teachings you have recently lived out in your own life.

Discuss Together

- What was it like to use Jesus' teachings to assess your Christian community and yourself? For example, did it make you uncomfortable, help you to recognize goodness you had overlooked, or shift your perspective in some way?

- Describe how you have recently witnessed Jesus' teachings being lived out among others in your own Christian community. What stood out most about it? How did it impact the people involved?

- Share an example of how you have recently lived out Jesus' teachings in your own life. What made this easy or difficult for you to do?

- If you could choose just one teaching and know that everyone in your Christian community would live it out fully and radically, which teaching would you choose? What do you imagine might happen — within and beyond your community — as a result?

✓ ✗	TEN REVOLUTIONARY TEACHINGS OF JESUS	
	Embrace a surrendered and sacrificial life.	If any of you wants to be my follower, you must turn from your selfish ways, take up your cross daily, and follow me. If you try to hang on to your life, you will lose it. But if you give up your life for my sake, you will save it (Luke 9:23–24 NLT).
	Love your enemies.	You have heard people say, "Love your neighbors and hate your enemies." But I tell you to love your enemies and pray for anyone who mistreats you (Matthew 5:43–44 CEV).
	Do not take revenge; turn the other cheek.	You have heard the law that says the punishment must match the injury: 'An eye for an eye, and a tooth for a tooth.' But I say, do not resist an evil person! If someone slaps you on the right cheek, offer the other cheek also (Matthew 5:38–39 NLT). If someone takes unfair advantage of you, use the occasion to practice the servant life. No more tit-for-tat stuff. Live generously (Matthew 5:42 MSG).
	Forgive— without ceasing.	Forgive, and you will be forgiven (Luke 6:37). Even if they sin against you seven times in a day and seven times come back to you saying "I repent," you must forgive them (Luke 17:4).
	Share the best of who you are and what you have with those who can't reciprocate.	When you give a banquet, invite the poor, the crippled, the lame, the blind, and you will be blessed. Although they cannot repay you, you will be repaid at the resurrection of the righteous (Luke 14:13–14).

	Do not worry.	I tell you not to worry about your life.... Can worry make you live longer? (Matthew 6:25, 27 CEV). Give your entire attention to what God is doing right now, and don't get worked up about what may or may not happen tomorrow (Matthew 6:34 MSG).
	Practice servanthood— it is the path to greatness.	Now that I, your Lord and Teacher, have washed your feet, you also should wash one another's feet (John 13:14). Whoever wants to become great among you must be your servant, and whoever wants to be first must be your slave—just as the Son of Man did not come to be served, but to serve, and to give his life as a ransom for many (Matthew 20:26–28).
	Protect yourself from greed.	Take care! Protect yourself against the least bit of greed. Life is not defined by what you have, even when you have a lot (Luke 12:15 MSG). Don't store up treasures here on earth, where moths eat them and rust destroys them, and where thieves break in and steal.... You cannot serve both God and money (Matthew 6:19, 24 NLT).
	Do not judge or condemn.	Do not judge, and you will not be judged. Do not condemn, and you will not be condemned (Luke 6:37).
	Humble yourself.	God blesses those who are humble, for they will inherit the whole earth (Matthew 5:5 NLT). If you put yourself above others, you will be put down. But if you humble yourself, you will be honored (Luke 14:11 CEV).

The Personal Question

4. At the end of the video, John posed this question: *How would you like Jesus to impact your life?* Focusing on your desires and hopes, how would you answer John's question? How would you most like Jesus to shape the person you are becoming?

5. The four remaining sessions in *Who Is This Man?* explore Jesus' inescapable influence on the world, and how we can advance — or impede — that influence through our own lives. In addition to learning together as a group, it's important to be aware of how God is at work among you — especially in how you relate to each other and share your lives throughout the study. As you discuss the teaching in each session, there will be many opportunities to speak life-giving — and life-challenging — words, and to listen to one another deeply.

   Take a few moments to consider the kinds of things that are important to you in this setting. What do you need or want from the other members of the group? Use one or more of the sentence starters on page 19, or your own statement, to help the group understand the best way to be a good companion to you throughout this study. As each person responds, use the chart on pages 20 – 21 to briefly note what is important to that person and how you can be a good companion to them.

It really helps me when ...

I tend to withdraw or feel anxious when ...

I'd like you to challenge me about ...

I'll know this group is a safe place if you ...

In our discussions, the best thing you could do for me is ...

NAME	THE BEST WAY I CAN BE A GOOD COMPANION TO THIS PERSON ...

NAME	THE BEST WAY I CAN BE A GOOD COMPANION TO THIS PERSON ...

Individual Activity: **What I Want to Remember** (2 Minutes)

Complete this activity on your own.

1. Briefly review the outline and any notes you took.
2. In the space below, write down the most significant thing you gained in this session — from the teaching, activities, or discussions.

   What I want to remember from this session ...

Closing Prayer

Close your time together with prayer.

Personal Study

● Read and Learn

Read chapters 1 – 3 of the book *Who Is This Man?* Use the space below to note any insights or questions you want to bring to the next group session.

● Study and Reflect

Humility, which was scorned in the ancient world, became enshrined in a cross and was eventually championed as a virtue.

Enemies, who were thought to be worthy of vengeance ("help your friends and punish your enemies"), came to be seen as worthy of love.

Forgiveness moved from weakness to an act of moral beauty.

Who Is This Man?, page 16

1. Jesus' teachings constantly challenged the prevailing values in ancient culture — in society at large and also within his own faith community (Matthew 7:28 – 29; John 7:15, 46). More than two thousand years after his death, Jesus' teachings are still revolutionary, challenging the prevailing values of both secular and religious cultures.

   • Turn to the Ten Revolutionary Teachings of Jesus chart from the group discussion (pages 16 – 17).

   • Review the teachings listed in the left column of the chart and circle the teaching that stands out most to you for any reason. Write it on the first row of the chart on page 25.

- Read the corresponding Scripture for the teaching you circled. Read it slowly, perhaps two or three times, and underline any words or phrases that resonate with you. Write your underlined words and phrases on the second line of the chart (page 25).

- Use the remaining questions on the chart to reflect on how this teaching connects with your life right now.

REFLECTING ON JESUS' TEACHING	
Which of Jesus' teachings stands out most to you?	
What words and phrases from Scripture resonate with you?	
What personal circumstances or problems come to mind in connection with this teaching?	
What relationships come to mind in connection with this teaching?	

Something about Jesus keeps prodding people to do what they would rather not: Francis of Assisi gives up his possessions, Augustine gives up his mistress, John Newton gives up his slave trade, and Father Damien gives up his health.

Who Is This Man?, page 18

2. As you reflect on your chart, what "prodding" are you aware of?

What reluctance, if any, do you feel about following through on this prodding?

If you were able to follow through, what good and redemptive thing do you hope might result — in your life and in the relationships you identified?

[Jesus] made history by starting in a humble place, in a spirit of love and acceptance, and allowing each person space to respond.

Who Is This Man?, page 12

3. There is nothing meek and mild about what Jesus taught. The writer of Hebrews leaves no room for doubt about this:

> God means what he says. What he says goes. His powerful Word is sharp as a surgeon's scalpel, cutting through everything, whether doubt or defense, laying us open to listen and obey. Nothing and no one is impervious to God's Word. We can't get away from it — no matter what. (Hebrews 4:12 – 13 MSG)

This passage states a vivid and sometimes painful truth, but it's rooted in the teachings of a Savior who always approaches us in a spirit of love and acceptance, inviting us to respond right where we are.

Where are you most aware of your need for love and acceptance from Jesus in connection with the teaching you've reflected on?

What do you sense Jesus' loving invitation to you might be?

● Guided Prayer

Lord, I am so grateful that love is the foundation for everything you want to teach me — even the hard lessons.

Today, I feel challenged by your teaching on ... This one is hard for me because ...

I believe you may be prompting me to ... What I need most from you now is ...

I want my life to be a reflection of your revolutionary love for me — this day and every day. Change me, Lord, and give me courage to live a radically different life because of love. Amen.

A REVOLUTION OF HUMANITY

[Jesus] created a new kind of human being, a fresh start for everybody. EPHESIANS 2:15 MSG

Group Discussion: Checking In (5 minutes)

A key part of getting to know God better is sharing your journey with others. Before watching the video, briefly check in with each other about your experiences since the last session. For example:

- What insights did you discover in the personal study or in the chapters you read from the book *Who Is This Man?*
- How did the last session impact your daily life or your relationship with God?
- What questions would you like to ask the other members of your group?

Video: A Revolution of Humanity (20 minutes)

Play the video segment for Session 2. As you watch, use the outline (pages 30 – 32) to follow along or to take notes on anything that stands out to you.

Notes

Jesus changed the way people think about the greatest and the least.

The people of Israel worshiped one God, who was loving and caring. Other ancient cultures had multiple gods and a hierarchical way of ordering life. Only the king was divine. Peasants and slaves were created by inferior gods. This is the Dignity Gap.

Jesus was heir to an explosive notion: *Every human being is made in the image of God. Every person has great worth.*

Jesus taught a totally different view of children.

Jesus modeled the worth God places on human life (Matthew 6:26; 10:29 – 31; 12:11 – 12).

Jesus created a whole new vision of what it means to be a human being — the revolutionary idea that the "least of these" were to be treasured.

Jesus had a radically new view of women.

We live in a different world today because of Jesus, regardless of what folks think about him.

This week:

- View everyone you encounter as an individual made in the image of God.

- Use the lens of human dignity and worth as you read the news.

- Consider traveling to a place where there are oppressed people, or use the Internet to learn more about people in need.

- Challenge yourself to think differently about people who are oppressed or in need. Pray for them.

- Invite God to use you to lift the dignity of another human being.

Group Discussion (33 minutes)

Take a few minutes to talk about what you just watched.

1. What part of the teaching had the most impact on you?

The Dignity Gap

2. The ancient, hierarchical way of establishing human dignity and worth was based on proximity to the gods — kings were thought to be divine or semi-divine and everyone else was created by a series of progressively lesser gods, ending with peasants and slaves at the bottom of the ladder.

- What hierarchies of human dignity and worth would you say are at work in our times and culture? What "proximities" do we tend to use to confer greater or lesser value on people?

- Consider one of your own spheres of life — for example, a group of friends, a social networking site, your workplace, school, church, or even this group. What are the subtle and not-so-subtle hierarchies of worth in this context? In other words, what makes someone a "king" or a "peasant"?

- In what ways, if any, have the hierarchies you described influenced how you view people, who you spend time with, or how you treat people?

Bestowed Worth and Dignity

3. Briefly describe a time when you were aware of being treated with dignity. Based on that experience, how would you complete this sentence?

   Treating someone with dignity means ...

4. When Jesus looked at people, he saw the image of God, and that is what caused him to treat each person with dignity.

   - How would you describe your own experience of being treated with dignity by Jesus?

- During the course of your everyday life, in what individuals or groups do you find it relatively easy to see the image of God? In what individuals or groups do you find it very difficult to see the image of God? Share the reasons for your response.

5. In a passage from the gospel of Luke, Jesus establishes the value of human beings using an analogy that is familiar to us now but would have been surprising in Jesus' day:

> Are not five sparrows sold for two pennies? Yet not one of them is forgotten by God.... Don't be afraid; you are worth more than many sparrows. (Luke 12:6 – 7)

Sparrows were cheap — buy-four-get-one-free. Worth less than a cent, they were among the humblest of temple sacrifices available to the poor.

- How does Jesus' use of sparrows challenge the prevailing hierarchy of human worth in the ancient world?

- How does Jesus' analogy impact you personally? For example, is it shocking, deeply reassuring, somewhat comforting, or so familiar it no longer has much impact?

- Would you say that your cultural context — one very different from that of Jesus' listeners — magnifies or diminishes the potential impact the analogy has on you? Why?

Dignity for the Least of These

6. In his teaching, Jesus often challenged the way people thought about the greatest and the least with statements like this:

> Anyone who welcomes a little child like this on my behalf welcomes me, and anyone who welcomes me also welcomes my Father who sent me. Whoever is the least among you is the greatest. (Luke 9:48 NLT)

The Greek word translated as "welcomes" is *dechomai* (dekh´-om-ahee). It can also be translated as "receive" or "accept" and is concerned primarily with hospitality — a very high value in Jesus' time and culture. Once when he was a dinner guest of a Pharisee, Jesus acknowledged three common acts of hospitality — washing feet, greeting with a kiss, pouring oil on the head — by pointing out how his host had failed at all three (Luke 7:44 – 46). The Pharisee may have invited Jesus to dinner, but he did not *welcome* Jesus.

- Have you ever experienced something like this — knowing you were included but somehow still not welcomed? How did it impact you?

- Among those considered the least of these in Jesus' day were children, women, prisoners, foreigners (non-Jews), and those who were sick or in need (Matthew 25:35 – 40). In the routines of your own life, with whom do you have contact who might be characterized as one of the "least of these" today?

- Jesus' revolutionary teaching was that the "least of these" were to be welcomed — received and accepted as persons of great worth and treated with dignity. How does this understanding of what it means to be welcoming challenge or encourage you in connection with the "least of these" in your own life?

Optional Group Discussion: Some of the "Least of These" in the World Today

If you have more than one hour, consider using this discussion as part of your meeting.

1. Go around the group and have a different person read aloud each of the ten statistics on pages 37 – 38. As the statistics are read, underline any words or phrases that stand out to you.

2. What are your initial reactions to what you've just heard and read? What stood out most to you?

3. How do you tend to respond to this kind of information about suffering in the world? For example, do you feel overwhelmed and hopeless, try to avoid it, or seek to learn more about it?

4. As individuals, we can't singlehandedly solve global problems, but that doesn't negate Jesus' command to welcome the "least of these." In what ways, if any, might your response to what you just heard change if you chose to be welcoming of the information itself—to receive it, accept it, and treat it with dignity?

Ten Statistics

- The poor in developing countries are disproportionately impacted by illegal detentions and overloaded legal systems. In India, there are eleven judges for every one million people. In the Philippines, the average judge has a backlog of 1,479 cases. Kenya has only sixty-three lawyer prosecutors for a population of 30 million. (*U.N. Commission on Legal Empowerment of the Poor; U.S. State Department*)

- At least one out of every three women in the world has been raped, beaten, coerced into sex, or otherwise violently abused in her lifetime. (*U.N. Development Fund for Women*)

- In the United States, 20.5 million Americans live in extreme poverty, which means annual cash income is half the poverty line — about $10,000 for a family of four. (*U.S. Census Bureau Report*)

- Eighty percent of human trafficking victims are women and girls. (*U.S. Department of State*)

- In the United States, 1.7 million children have a parent serving time in jail. (*Prison Fellowship International*)

- Seventy percent of the population in the Democratic Republic of the Congo is undernourished. (*Global Hunger Index*)

- There are an estimated 27 million slaves in the world today — more than any other time in history. (Kevin Bales, *Disposable People*)

- Worldwide, it is estimated that 16 million children under age eighteen have lost one or both parents to AIDS. Approximately 14.8 million of these children live in sub-Saharan Africa. (*UNAIDS Report on the Global AIDS Epidemic*)

- In the United States, 49.9 million people (16.3 percent of the population) do not have medical insurance. (*U.S. Census Bureau Report*)

- Even though women in rural areas produce between 60 and 80 percent of food in developing countries, they own less than 2 percent of the land. (*Oxfam*)

Sources: International Justice Mission (*IJM.org*); Prison Fellowship International (*pfi.org*); World Hunger Education Service (*worldhunger .org*); Avert (*avert.org*).

7. At the end of the group discussion for Session 1, you had the opportunity to share what you need from the other members of the group and to write down the best ways you can be good companions to one another (pages 20 – 21).

- Briefly restate what you asked for from the group in Session 1. What additions or clarifications would you like to make that would help the group know more about how to be a good companion to you? As each person responds, add any additional information to the chart on pages 20 – 21. (If you were absent from the last session, share your response to question 5 on pages 18 – 19. Then use the chart to write down what is important to each member of the group.)

- In what ways, if any, did you find yourself responding differently to other members of the group in this session based on what they asked for in the previous session? What made that easy or difficult for you to do?

Individual Activity: **What I Want to Remember** (2 Minutes)

Complete this activity on your own.

1. Briefly review the outline and any notes you took.
2. In the space below, write down the most significant thing you gained in this session — from the teaching, activities, or discussions.

   What I want to remember from this session ...

Closing Prayer

Close your time together with prayer.

Personal Study

● Read and Learn

Read chapters 4 – 6 of the book *Who Is This Man?* Use the space below to note any insights or questions you want to bring to the next group session.

● Study and Reflect

The idea that "the least of these" were to be treasured — that somehow the Jesus that they followed was present in despised suffering — was essentially a Copernican revolution of humanity. It created a new vision of the human being.

Who Is This Man?, page 39

---

1. Jesus eliminates all distinctions between the greatest and the least by aligning himself with "the least of these" — those who are hungry, thirsty, foreigners, naked, sick, imprisoned (Matthew 25:35 – 36). Or, in the poignant words of author David Bentley Hart:

   … the autistic or Down syndrome or otherwise disabled child … the derelict or wretched or broken man or woman who has wasted his or her life away; the homeless, the utterly impoverished, the diseased, the mentally ill, the physically disabled; exiles, refugees, fugitives; even criminals and reprobates.[1]

   By definition, the least of these are people who are overlooked, avoided, or looked down on. We tend not to see them.

---

1. David Bentley Hart, *Atheist Delusions* (Ann Arbor, Mich.: Sheridan Books, 2009), 214.

Use the list that follows to briefly reflect on the places you might be in the course of a typical week. As you imagine each setting and the people in it, ask yourself, "Is there an individual or group here who is routinely overlooked, avoided, or looked down on?" Place a checkmark next to those settings. If you find it difficult to identify anyone, review the list of ten statistics from the group discussion (pages 37 – 38) and choose one of these people groups as your focus.

☐ Home
☐ Workplace
☐ Neighborhood
☐ Church
☐ Small group
☐ School
☐ Coffee shop
☐ Restaurant
☐ Day care
☐ Commute or daily travels
☐ Fitness center
☐ Grocery store or other
   retail store

☐ Book club or other social
   group
☐ Sports league
☐ Dry cleaner
☐ Ministry or volunteer
   organization
☐ Play group
☐ Park
☐ Shopping mall
☐ Other:

Choose one of the locations you checked and circle it. Write a brief description or the name of the person or group you identified in that location.

What leads you to consider this person or group among the "least of these"?

Which of the three responses — overlooking, avoiding, or looking down on — best characterizes your response to this person or group? What is it about them that prompts this response in you?

Jesus' crankiness and compassion came from the same source: his outrageous love for every individual, and his pain when anyone is undervalued. In all the stories of Jesus' compassion, we are never told that he had compassion on someone because they deserved it. It was only because they were in need.

Who Is This Man?, page 37

---

2. Acceptance is an essential component of compassion and a defining characteristic of how Jesus understands greatness:

> [The disciples] started arguing over which of them would be most famous. When Jesus realized how much this mattered to them, he brought a child to his side. "Whoever accepts this child as if the child were me, accepts me," he said. "And whoever accepts me, accepts the One who sent me. You become great by accepting, not asserting. Your spirit, not your size, makes the difference." (Luke 9:46 – 48 MSG)

To *accept* is to receive what is offered or to say yes to an invitation. When you think of the person or group you identified in question 1, what is it they might be offering for your acceptance? What is the invitation they represent?

To *assert* is to insist on something or to exercise power. In what ways, if any, do you sense you might be asserting yourself in regard to this person or group? How might your assertion impact your ability to accept them?

The reason every person has great worth, for Jesus, is that every person is loved by God.
Who Is This Man?, **page 27**

---

3. Mother Teresa said, "I see Jesus in every human being. I say to myself, this is hungry Jesus, I must feed him. This is sick Jesus. This one has leprosy or gangrene; I must wash him and tend to him. I serve because I love Jesus."

   Take a moment to imagine Jesus in the guise of the person or group you identified in question 1. What resistance or shifts do you notice in yourself as you do this?

How might you adapt Mother Teresa's statement to apply to this person? For example, *This is friendless Jesus, I must welcome him, enjoy him.*

What thoughts or emotions does your statement make you aware of?

Every human being has royal dignity. When Jesus looked at people, he saw the image of God. He saw this in everyone. It caused him to treat each person with dignity.
Who Is This Man?, **page 26**

---

4. When Jesus treated people with dignity, it often came at the expense of his own. Consider, for example, when he spent time with social outcasts, washed the disciples' feet, or surrendered himself to a shameful execution.

   As you think about lifting the dignity of the person you identified in question 1, what part of your dignity might you have to let go of?

● Guided Prayer

Lord, thank you for accepting me in all of my "least of these" moments — all the times I would be easy to overlook, avoid, or look down on. Where would I be without your love and acceptance?

I want to see your image in every person in my life, but it's so hard sometimes. I especially struggle with ...

I know that investing in the dignity of others may cost me some of my own. I sense you may be asking me to let go of ... To do this, I need ...

You have never offered me less than radical acceptance and grace. In your mercy, remove from me every impulse to overlook, avoid, or look down on the people you love so much. Amen.

THE POWER OF FORGIVENESS

Our love for our enemies shows to whom we really belong. It shows our true home.

HENRI J. M. NOUWEN,
LETTERS TO MARC ABOUT JESUS

Group Discussion: Checking In (5 minutes)

A key part of getting to know God better is sharing your journey with others. Before watching the video, briefly check in with each other about your experiences since the last session. For example:

- What insights did you discover in the personal study or in the chapters you read from the book *Who Is This Man?*
- How did the last session impact your daily life or your relationship with God?
- What questions would you like to ask the other members of your group?

Video: The Power of Forgiveness (22 minutes)

Play the video segment for Session 3. As you watch, use the outline (pages 48 – 49) to follow along or to take notes on anything that stands out to you.

Notes

Forgiveness is not a natural act.

How to distinguish between forgiveness and reconciliation:

Forgiveness is letting go of my right to hurt you back.

Reconciliation requires the sincere intentions of both parties.

I am called to love the repentant person who has hurt me; and I am also called to love the unrepentant person.

Love of enemies is Jesus' teaching that is most famous and perhaps most violated, even in our day.

We human beings are side-takers. We divide the human race into us versus them.

For Jesus, it's not *us* and *them*. It's *perfect* and *not perfect*; *holy* and *sinful*. Which puts all of humanity on the same side.

This week:

- Identify someone in your life whom you regard as "them" or as being on the other side.

- Consider what it would mean in practical terms for you to be with them and care for them. Invite Jesus to call you over to the other side.

Group Discussion (31 minutes)

Take a few minutes to talk about what you just watched.

1. What part of the teaching had the most impact on you?

Mary and Oshea

2. Here is how John described the difference between
   forgiveness and reconciliation:
      Forgiveness: letting go of the right to hurt someone back
      Reconciliation: restoration of relationship that requires the
   sincere intentions of both parties

   • How do you recognize these dynamics at work in both
     Mary and Oshea?

   • If you could have a conversation with Mary about
     forgiveness and reconciliation, what would you most like
     to ask her? Why?

3. Mary began her first conversation with Oshea by saying, "I
   don't really know you. You don't really know me. Let's just
   start there." It was Mary's willingness to understand Oshea's
   side of what happened that made it possible for Oshea to
   acknowledge what he'd taken from Mary.

- What do you find most challenging or most encouraging about what Mary did?

- Think of a time when you were on Oshea's side of the forgiveness equation — you had wronged someone and damaged the relationship. How do you imagine you would have responded if the person you had wronged approached you with a sincere interest in wanting to understand your side of what happened?

Loving the Other Side

4. Forgiveness is not a natural act. Jesus was citing conventional wisdom when he noted:

> You have heard that it was said, "Love your neighbor and hate your enemy." But I tell you, love your enemies and pray for those who persecute you, that you may be children of your Father in heaven. He causes his sun to rise on the evil and the good, and sends rain on the righteous and the unrighteous. (Matthew 5:43 – 45)

Jesus is speaking here about personal enemies, about relationships marked by mutual hostility or hatred. The Greek word he uses for his command to *love* is *agapao* — the verb form of *agape* — which is the kind of love God has for us. In essence, the command is, *Love your enemies the way God loves you.* Why? Because God doesn't take sides.

- How do you typically respond when you read Bible passages such as this one from Matthew or hear them taught in church? For example, do you tend to feel guilty and resistant or affirmed and encouraged? Why?

- As hard as it might be to live out this teaching in a difficult relationship, is there anything about going to "the other side" that excites you or stirs up hope in you? How do you imagine it might be life-giving for you?

5. Think of someone who feels like an enemy or who represents "the other side" to you.

   - Without naming the person, briefly describe what you think they might say about how you treat them.

   - In what ways, if any, does thinking about your behavior from their side shift your perspective on the relationship?

- What thoughts or emotions are you aware of when you consider the possibility of approaching this person as Mary did Oshea — initiating a conversation, seeking to understand their side, cultivating compassion for that person?

6. Take a few moments to reflect on what you've learned and experienced together in this study so far.

   - How has learning more about Jesus' influence on the world over the last two thousand years impacted you?

   - Since the first session, what shifts have you noticed in yourself in terms of how you relate to the group? For example, do you feel more or less guarded, understood, challenged, encouraged, connected, etc.?

   - What adjustments, if any, would you like to make to the Session 1 chart (pages 20 – 21) that would help other members of the group know how to be better companions for you?

Individual Activity: What I Want to Remember (2 Minutes)

Complete this activity on your own.

1. Briefly review the outline and any notes you took.
2. In the space below, write down the most significant thing you gained in this session — from the teaching, activities, or discussions.

   What I want to remember from this session ...

Closing Prayer

Close your time together with prayer.

Personal Study

● Read and Learn

Read chapters 7 – 9 of the book *Who Is This Man?* Use the space below to note any insights or questions you want to bring to the next group session.

● Study and Reflect

We human beings are side-takers. We all tend to divide the human race into *us* versus *them*. This happens for religious reasons but can also happen because of ethnicity, culture, and language. Two of the most powerful words in the human race are *us* and *them*.
Who Is This Man?, pages 92 – 93

---

1. There are an endless number of things over which we take sides — *we are conservative, they are liberal; we are Jews, they are Arabs; we are black, they are white; we are educated, they are not; we are the 99 percent, they are the 1 percent; we are Protestants, they are Catholics; we are progressives, they are traditionalists.* And the list goes on and on.

   When you think of the people in your life through the lens of *us* and *them*, who comes to mind on the *us* side, and who comes to mind on the *them* side? Use the first row of the chart (page 56) to write down three to five names for each side. Use the remaining questions on the chart to reflect on your experiences of both sides.

QUESTIONS	US	THEM
What names come to mind?		
What labels do you tend to use when you think about the people on each side? For example, liberal/ conservative, Christian/ atheist, popular/ unpopular, etc.		
How do you feel when you are around these people? For example, relaxed, cautious, defensive, accepted, etc.		
What are your most characteristic behaviors around these people? For example, joking around, silent treatment, avoidance, showing interest/ concern, etc.		

2. Briefly review what you wrote on your chart. What stands out most to you about yourself? For example, what insights do the things you wrote in each column provide about who you are or what is important to you?

In what ways do the people on the *us* side bring out the best in you?

In what ways do the people on the *them* side bring out the worst in you?

For Jesus, the categories break down like this: It's not us and them. It's *perfect* and *not perfect*. It's *holy* and *sinful*. Which puts all of humanity on the same side: the wrong side. But Jesus was determined to make that *his* side.

Who Is This Man?, page 96

---

3. *The Message* provides a compelling perspective on Jesus' familiar teaching about loving enemies:

You're familiar with the old written law, "Love your friend," and its unwritten companion, "Hate your enemy." I'm challenging that. I'm telling you to love your enemies. Let them bring out the best in you, not the worst. When someone gives you a hard time, respond with the energies of prayer, for then you are working out of your true selves, your God-created selves. This is what God does. He gives his best — the sun to warm and the rain to nourish — to everyone, regardless: the good and bad, the nice and nasty. (Matthew 5:43 – 45 MSG)

How would you describe yourself when you are giving your best — working out of your God-created self? Write down three to five words or phrases. For example, *I am thoughtful, diligent, and loyal.*

For each word or phrase you wrote down, consider what it might mean to invest that quality into the relationships with the people in the *them* column on your chart. How could you begin to give your best — your God-created self — to those relationships?

● Guided Prayer

God, thank you for all the ways you give your best to me — from beauty in the world around me to love and grace that will not let me go.

I confess that I am a side-taker. It's often hard for me to give my best to people who bring out the worst in me. What makes this especially challenging for me is ...

I want to see all of my relationships the way you do — on the same side. I ask for your help with the people on my "them" list. Specifically, I need wisdom and guidance about ...

Every side is your side, Lord. I believe it with all my heart. Help me to live it out in all my relationships. Amen.

WHY IT'S A SMALL WORLD AFTER ALL

It takes all sorts to make a world; or a church.

C. S. LEWIS, *LETTERS TO MALCOLM*

Group Discussion: Checking In (5 minutes)

A key part of getting to know God better is sharing your journey with others. Before watching the video, briefly check in with each other about your experiences since the last session. For example:

- What insights did you discover in the personal study or in the chapters you read from the book *Who Is This Man?*
- How did the last session impact your daily life or your relationship with God?
- What questions would you like to ask the other members of your group?

Video: Why It's a Small World after All (21 minutes)

Play the video segment for Session 4. As you watch, use the outline (pages 62 – 64) to follow along or to take notes on anything that stands out to you.

Notes

Jesus picked some people at random, and they were about as much use to him as a hole in the head. The Bible's word for this is *election* — the annoying bride of Christ.

Jesus recruited his disciples, which was unusual for a rabbi. It reflects an idea deeply embedded in Jewish life: that calling begins with God.

Jesus' followers formed an alternative community. They rearranged their way of life (Acts 2:45 – 48).

They came to understand themselves to have a mission or calling. Their calling was to:

- Form a community that reflected the presence and power of God
- Extend the love of this community to everyone
- Invite anyone who was interested to join them

The idea of conversion came to the world through Jesus.

Before Jesus, where was there a movement that actively sought to include every single human being — regardless of nationality, ethnicity, status, wealth, gender, moral background, education?

Imagine a world with no church ...

What would our world be like if Jesus hadn't invited that little group of people to follow him?

The church is God's dream for the redemptive togetherness of the human race.

This week:

- Pray this prayer: *Jesus, what would you like the church to look like? How can I be a part of that?*

- If you're *not* a part of a church, consider what it would be like if you were part of one.

- If you *are* a part of a church, consider how you can make it a place of greater beauty and joy. Seek to make peace. Join with friends to minister to the people around you — those who need education, who are hungry, or in prison.

Group Discussion (32 minutes)

Take a few minutes to talk about what you just watched.

1. What part of the teaching had the most impact on you?

Chosen and Called

2. A unique perspective in Judeo-Christian teaching is the idea that calling begins with God. God takes initiative with Israel:

> I am the LORD, the holy God. You have been chosen to be my people, and so you must be holy too. (Leviticus 20:26 CEV)

And Jesus takes initiative with his disciples:

> You did not choose me. I chose you and sent you out to produce fruit, the kind of fruit that will last. (John 15:16 CEV)

Everything in the spiritual life begins with God — from our very breath (Isaiah 42:5) to our ability to love (1 John 4:19).

- How have you experienced God's initiative in your relationship with him? For example, how did God take the first step in your journey of coming to faith, in preparing you for service, or in leading you to take an action you might not otherwise have taken?

- Where are you most aware of God taking initiative with you right now? For example, is it in shaping the person you are becoming, prompting you in your relationships, or leading you to take a God-honoring risk?

- To be chosen is to be called for a purpose. God chooses Israel *for* the world, not *instead* of it, which is why the Scriptures declare, "All nations will be blessed through you" (Galatians 3:8; Genesis 22:18). Jesus chooses his disciples for the purpose of bearing fruit.

  When you consider your own Christian community — people you know, care about, worship with — how would you describe the way the community lives out its purpose? What characterizes this community as a group of individuals who are *for* the world, and bearing fruit that will last?

An Alternative Community

3. Jesus' followers were ordinary people who rearranged their lives in radical ways:

> They spent their time learning from the apostles, and they were like family to each other. They also broke bread and prayed together. Everyone was amazed by the many miracles and wonders that the apostles worked. All the Lord's followers often met together, and they shared everything they had. They would sell their property and possessions and give the money to whoever needed it. Day after day they met together in the temple. They broke bread together in different homes and shared their food happily and freely, while praising God. Everyone liked them, and each day the Lord added to their group others who were being saved. (Acts 2:42 – 47 CEV)

- The first believers formed an alternative community — they spent their time, used their resources, conducted their relationships, and worshiped God in unconventional ways.

   Which number on the continuum would you say best describes the degree to which your Christian community could be characterized as alternative? Share the reasons for your choice.

1 2 3 4 5 6 7 8 9 10

Not at all   Somewhat   Extremely
alternative   alternative   alternative

- Within your local setting and culture, what would you identify as some of the essential characteristics of an alternative Christian community? Consider the same categories described above — time, resources, relationships, and worship.

God's Dream for the Church

4. On the video, John pointed out that the idea behind Disney's "It's a Small World" ride — of a diverse world gathered together like a family — is an idea that originated with Jesus. It's interesting to note that the ride began as "Children of the World," an attraction PEPSI hired Walt Disney to develop for the 1964 New York World's Fair. Conceived as a tribute and fundraiser for UNICEF, the original design called for the national anthems of every country featured throughout the ride to be played simultaneously. Anticipating a loud racket of competing words and melodies, Disney asked two songwriters to create one song that could be easily translated into many languages and played as a round. The result was "It's a Small World after All."

   - As Jesus' followers, what kinds of things would you say we do that cause our presence in the world to be more like a loud racket of competing words and melodies rather than one song? How do you recognize these things in yourself and in your own Christian community?

- God's dream for the church is that we sing one song, and that every single human being — regardless of nationality, ethnicity, status, wealth, gender, moral background, or education — be included, loved, and transformed in the process. Within your own Christian community, where would you say Jesus' followers *are* singing one song — living out God's dream for the church?

5. Briefly touch base with each other about how you're doing in the group. Use one of the sentence starters below, or your own statement, to help group members learn more about how to be good companions to you.

   I want to give you permission to challenge me more about …

   An area where I really need your help or sensitivity is …

   It always helps me to feel more connected to the group when …

   Something I've learned about myself because of this group is …

Individual Activity: What I Want to Remember (2 Minutes)

Complete this activity on your own.

1. Briefly review the outline and any notes you took.
2. In the space below, write down the most significant thing you gained in this session — from the teaching, activities, or discussions.

   What I want to remember from this session ...

Closing Prayer

Close your time together with prayer.

GET A HEAD START ON THE DISCUSSION FOR SESSION 5

As part of the group discussion for Session 5, you'll have an opportunity to talk about what you've learned and experienced together throughout the *Who Is This Man?* study. Between now and your next meeting, take a few moments to review the previous sessions and identify the teaching, discussions, or activities that stand out most to you. Use the worksheet on pages 70–71 to briefly summarize the highlights of what you've learned and experienced.

Session 5 Head Start Worksheet

Using the space provided, reflect on what you've learned and experienced throughout the *Who Is This Man?* study. You may want to review notes from the video teaching, what you wrote down for "What I Want to Remember" at the end of each group session, responses in the personal studies, etc. Here are some questions you might consider as part of your review:

- What insights did I gain from this session?

- What was the most important thing I learned about myself in this session?

- How did I experience God's presence or leading related to this session?

- How did this session impact my relationships with the other people in the group?

Session 1 The Man Who Won't Go Away (pages 11 – 28)

Session 2: A Revolution of Humanity (pages 29–45)

Session 3: The Power of Forgiveness (pages 47–59)

Session 4: Why It's a Small World after All (pages 61–77)

Personal Study

● Read and Learn

Read chapters 10 – 12 of the book *Who Is This Man?* Use the space below to note any insights or questions you want to bring to the next group session.

● Study and Reflect

This little group of people who followed Jesus formed a kind of alternative community. They rearranged their way of life. They met together daily. They learned from the teachings of Jesus passed down to his disciples, they prayed, they served, they "ate together with glad and sincere hearts." They gave whatever possessions they had to help each other. And as for outsiders, in the memorable translation of Eugene Peterson, "People in general liked what they saw" (Acts 2:47 MSG).

Who Is This Man?, page 129

---

1. The New Testament features several metaphors to describe the alternative community created by Jesus' followers. Among them are:

    * *A flock* (Luke 12:32; Acts 20:28; 1 Peter 5:2)

    * *The body of Christ* (Romans 12:4 – 5; 1 Corinthians 12:27; Colossians 1:24)

    * *The bride of Christ* (2 Corinthians 11:2; Ephesians 5:31 – 32; Revelation 19:7 – 8)

- *God's family* (2 Corinthians 6:18; Ephesians 2:19;
  1 Timothy 5:1 – 2)

- *A spiritual house or temple* (Hebrews 3:6; 1 Peter 2:4 – 5;
  1 Timothy 3:14 – 15)

Choose one of the metaphors that interests you and look up the associated passages in your Bible.

What do you find intriguing about this metaphor for Christian community?

In what way would you say this picture of Christian community represents something you want to experience but haven't, or want to experience more fully?

2. Jesus' followers in the early church were ordinary people who rearranged their lives in radical ways:

> They committed themselves to the teaching of the apostles, the life together, the common meal, and the prayers.
>
> Everyone around was in awe — all those wonders and signs done through the apostles! And all the believers lived in a wonderful harmony, holding everything in common. They sold whatever they owned and pooled their resources so that each person's need was met.
>
> They followed a daily discipline of worship in the Temple followed by meals at home, every meal a celebration, exuberant and joyful, as they praised God. People in general

liked what they saw. Every day their number grew as God added those who were saved. (Acts 2:42 – 47 MSG)

Read through the passage once more, this time as if it were a description of your Christian community. Pause over each phrase and try to imagine what it would be like to share these experiences with the people you know. Use the prompts below to write down any ideas, emotions, or images that come to mind.

Teaching/learning ...

Life together ...

A common meal (the Lord's Supper) ...

Prayers ...

Awe and harmony ...

Shared resources ...

Worship ...

Joyous meals in homes ...

Praising God ...

Goodwill ...

Lives saved ...

Which of the phrases, if any, were you aware of feeling resistant to? What is it that makes you uncomfortable about it?

Which of the phrases stand out as something you would most like to experience in your community? How do you hope it would impact you and the people you care about?

Jesus started small. Often his followers are at their best doing small things.

Who Is This Man?, page 135

3. Everything the Acts 2 community did was fueled by love — love of God and love of others. They rearranged their lives around that love and experienced it as joy.

   Take a moment to bring to mind the names and faces in your own Christian community. As you look at each one through the lens of love, what is your attention drawn to?

"We can't all do great things," said Mother Teresa, "but we can do small things with great love." What small thing do you sense God may be inviting you to do with great love?

● Guided Prayer

God, thank you for loving me and for calling me into a community that reflects your love.

When I think about my experiences in Christian community, I am aware of disappointments and failures — my own and others. I confess to some disillusionment and even cynicism. As far as I am able, I surrender these things to you and ask for your healing for ...

Help me to see everyone in my community through the eyes of love, especially ... I sense you may be inviting me to ...

Change my heart, Lord. Give me the power and the desire to rearrange my life for love of you. Amen.

THREE DAYS THAT CHANGED THE WORLD

They took him down from the cross and buried him. And then God raised him from death. There is no disputing that.   ACTS 13:29 – 31 MSG

Group Discussion: Checking In (5 minutes)

A key part of getting to know God better is sharing your journey with others. Before watching the video, briefly check in with each other about your experiences since the last session. For example:

- What insights did you discover in the personal study or in the chapters you read from the book *Who Is This Man?*

- How did the last session impact your daily life or your relationship with God?

- What questions would you like to ask the other members of your group?

Video: Three Days That Changed the World (21 minutes)

Play the video segment for Session 5. As you watch, use the outline (pages 80–82) to follow along or to take notes on anything that stands out to you.

Notes

How did it happen that Jesus — a great teacher and exemplary human being — ends up being executed as an enemy of the state?

Jesus' death is central to his story in an unusual way. It takes up about one-third of each of the four Gospels.

Two thousand years later, his death is the most important, most remembered death in the history of the world. And the cross is the most widely recognized symbol on earth.

Jesus died on the cross on Friday. Then came Saturday — the only day in the last two thousand years when literally not one person in the world believed Jesus was alive.

Why is there a Saturday?

Saturday is the day when nothing happens — nothing but silence.

The miracle of Sunday is that a dead man lives. The miracle of Saturday is that the eternal Son of God lays dead. Jesus defeats our great enemy death not by proclaiming his invincibility over it, but by submitting himself to it.

Sunday changed everything, but not in the way many people think.

These three days form the hinge of history: Friday when he died; Saturday, the day of silence and waiting; Sunday, the day of hope.

Has the hope Jesus released become your hope? The invitation: "Come and see" (John 1:46).

Group Discussion (32 minutes)

Take a few minutes to talk about what you just watched.

1. What part of the teaching had the most impact on you?

Friday: Choosing the Cross

2. In facing his death, Jesus wasn't a victim of forces beyond his control — he had options. He could fight like the zealots, withdraw like the Essenes, collaborate with the chief priests, cut a deal with Pilate, or call on God to be delivered.

Instead, he chose to die out of love for others. Here is how he explained it to his disciples:

> I am the good shepherd. The good shepherd sacrifices his life for the sheep.... The Father loves me because I sacrifice my life so I may take it back again. No one can take my life from me. I sacrifice it voluntarily. For I have the authority to lay it down when I want to and also to take it up again. For this is what my Father has commanded. (John 10:11, 17–18 NLT)

Why do you think it matters so much that Jesus' disciples understand that he is making a sacrificial choice from a position of authority?

3. After predicting his own death, Jesus uses the means of his death — a cross — to describe the sacrificial choice he expects his followers to make:

> Then he said to the crowd, "If any of you wants to be my follower, you must turn from your selfish ways, take up your cross daily, and follow me. If you try to hang on to your life, you will lose it. But if you give up your life for my sake, you will save it." (Luke 9:23–24 NLT)

We may suffer many things in life, but they aren't necessarily crosses. By Jesus' definition, a cross is only a cross if you choose it. It is a decision made from a position of authority — you could choose otherwise, but you don't. For love of Christ, you crawl up on the altar and consent to die — to self-will, self-gratification, self-protection — daily.

- How do you recognize the distinction between suffering and taking up your cross in your own life? For example, what are the unique demands of each? What are the unique ways that each has the potential to increase or diminish faith and spiritual growth?

- Do you think it's possible to take an experience of suffering (something we did not choose) and allow it to become a cross — something we choose and submit to for love of Christ? Share the reasons for your response.

- Jesus describes taking up one's cross as a *daily* choice, a habit practiced in the routines of everyday life and relationships. As you think back over the last day or two, what opportunities did you have to take up your cross — to make a loving, sacrificial choice? How did you respond? What happened as a result?

Saturday: Waiting

4. On the video, John said, "From heaven's standpoint, I wonder if the greater miracle isn't Saturday. The miracle of Saturday is the eternal Son of God lays dead. He defeats our great enemy death not by proclaiming his invincibility over it, but by submitting himself to it."

If Saturday in Jesus' story is also a miracle, what implications do you think it has for us as Jesus' followers? In the life of faith, what would you say is the miracle of the fallow, silent, in-between times?

5. All three-day stories share a structure. On the first day there is trouble, on the third day there is deliverance; on the second day, there is nothing. Silence.

- As you look back over your life, are there experiences or seasons you would describe as a three-day story? Within that experience, how would you characterize "Saturday" — the time of continued trouble, silence, and confusion?

- In what ways, if any, would you say you are in a Saturday season now? How would you characterize your response to it — as despair, denial, waiting, or something else?

Sunday: Hope to Die For

6. Jesus released a new kind of hope — hope that called people to die to the lesser life of a lesser self so that a greater self might be born.

   Where are you most aware of a need for this kind of hope in your life right now? What lesser thing do you sense God may be asking you to die to?

7. Discuss what you've learned and experienced together throughout the *Who Is This Man?* study.

   • What would you say is the most significant thing you learned about Jesus and his influence on the world? How has what you've learned impacted you (for example, in your attitudes, behaviors, relationships, etc.)?

   • How have you recognized God at work in your life through this study? What do you sense God's invitation to you might be?

- At the end of every session, you had an opportunity to talk about what you needed from the other members of the group and how you could be good companions for one another. What changes, if any, have you noticed in the ways you interact with each other now compared to the beginning of the study?

Individual Activity: **What I Want to Remember** (2 Minutes)

Complete this activity on your own.

1. Briefly review the outline and any notes you took.
2. In the space below, write down the most significant thing you gained in this session — from the teaching, activities, or discussions.

   What I want to remember from this session ...

Closing Prayer

Close your time together with prayer.

Personal Study

● Read and Learn

Read chapters 13 – 15 of the book *Who Is This Man?* Use the space below to note any insights or questions you want to discuss with a group member or friend in the coming days.

● Study and Reflect

The cross is a reminder that there is something in me that needs to die.... The resurrection hope is the hope that lies on the other side of dying.

Who Is This Man?, **page 192**

1. Jesus uses the metaphor of seeds to describe the purpose of his own death and the way of life he wants his followers to embrace:

   I tell you the truth, unless a kernel of wheat is planted in the soil and dies, it remains alone. But its death will produce many new kernels — a plentiful harvest of new lives. Those who love their life in this world will lose it. Those who care nothing for their life in this world will keep it for eternity. Anyone who wants to be my disciple must follow me, because my servants must be where I am. And the Father will honor anyone who serves me. (John 12:24 – 26 NLT)

For a fresh perspective on this familiar passage, read it again from *The Message*:

> Listen carefully: Unless a grain of wheat is buried in the ground, dead to the world, it is never any more than a grain of wheat. But if it is buried, it sprouts and reproduces itself many times over. In the same way, anyone who holds on to life just as it is destroys that life. But if you let it go, reckless in your love, you'll have it forever, real and eternal. If any of you wants to serve me, then follow me. Then you'll be where I am, ready to serve at a moment's notice. The Father will honor and reward anyone who serves me. (John 12:24–26 MSG)

A grain of wheat is an embryonic plant. In its immature state, it is not bad — so that putting it in the soil might be construed a punishment — but it is limited. Use the prompts that follow (pages 90–91) to reflect on any grains of wheat in your own life. What are you aware of in this area of life that keeps you in an immature state or limits you in some way?

My pace of life ...

My finances ...

My relationships ...

My body ...

My plans ...

My needs ...

Other ...

2. Of all the things you wrote down in answer to question 1, of which do you feel most protective? In other words, where do you feel most determined to "hold on to life just as it is"? What are you most afraid of losing?

What is this attachment costing you? Or, how is your unwillingness to let go causing you to lose or damage some aspect of your life?

What comes to mind when you imagine being "reckless in your love" and letting it go?

93

What got released on Sunday was hope. Not hope that life would turn out well. Not even hope that there will be life after death. Hope that called people to die: die to selfishness and sin and fear and greed. Die to the lesser life of a lesser self so that a greater self might be born.

Who Is This Man?, page 190

3. If you were able to die to this aspect of your life — to let it go for love of Christ — what is the harvest you hope for?

● Guided Prayer

Jesus, thank you that the foundation of my faith is your reckless, sacrificial love for me.

As I think about the things I need to let go of, I feel resistant or afraid because ...

Please help me to trust that there will be a greater life if I am able to let go of my lesser life. I especially ask for help letting go of ... because ...

Lord, I want to follow wherever you lead me — to be where you are every day, ready to serve at a moment's notice. Ready to surrender my life for love of you. Amen.

Who Is This Man?

The Unpredictable Impact of the Inescapable Jesus

John Ortberg

Jesus' impact on our world is highly unlikely, widely inescapable, largely unknown, and decidedly double-edged. It is unlikely in light of the severe limitations of his earthly life; it is inescapable because of the range of impact; it is unknown because history doesn't connect dots; and it is doubled-edged because his followers have wreaked so much havoc, often in his name.

He is history's most familiar figure, yet he is the man no one knows. His impact on the world is immense and non-accidental. From the Dark Ages to post-modernity, he is the Man who won't go away.

And yet ... you can miss him in historical lists for many reasons, maybe the most obvious being the way he lived his life. He did not loudly and demonstrably defend his movement in the spirit of a rising political or military leader. He did not lay out a case that history would judge his brand of belief superior in all future books.

His life and teaching simply drew people to follow him. He made history by starting in a humble place, in a spirit of love and acceptance, and allowing each person space to respond.

His vision of life continues to haunt and challenge humanity. His influence has swept over history bringing inspiration to what has happened in art, science, government, medicine, and education; he has taught humans about dignity, compassion, forgiveness, and hope.

Available in stores and online!

Share Your Thoughts

With the Author: Your comments will be forwarded to the author when you send them to *zauthor@zondervan.com*.

With Zondervan: Submit your review of this book by writing to *zreview@zondervan.com*.

Free Online Resources at
www.zondervan.com

Zondervan AuthorTracker: Be notified whenever your favorite authors publish new books, go on tour, or post an update about what's happening in their lives at www.zondervan.com/authortracker.

Daily Bible Verses and Devotions: Enrich your life with daily Bible verses or devotions that help you start every morning focused on God. Visit www.zondervan.com/newsletters.

Free Email Publications: Sign up for newsletters on Christian living, academic resources, church ministry, fiction, children's resources, and more. Visit www.zondervan.com/newsletters.

Zondervan Bible Search: Find and compare Bible passages in a variety of translations at www.zondervanbiblesearch.com.

Other Benefits: Register to receive online benefits like coupons and special offers, or to participate in research.

ZONDERVAN.com/
AUTHORTRACKER
follow your favorite authors